How
for Your Pet

Dr. Amy Cousino

Strategic Book Publishing
New York, New York

Copyright 2009
All rights reserved — Dr. Amy Cousino

Book Design: Stacie Tingen

No part of this book may be reproduced or transmitted in any form or by any means, graphic, electronic, or mechanical, including photocopying, recording, taping, or by any information storage retrieval system, without the permission, in writing, from the publisher.

Strategic Book Publishing
An imprint of Writers Literary & Publishing Services, Inc.
845 Third Avenue, 6th Floor — #6016
New York, NY 10022
www.StrategicBookPublishing.com

ISBN: 978-1-60693-375-6
SKU: 1-60693-375-2

Copyright 2007 by Amy Cousino, DVM., Author, rev. 2008.
All rights reserved under International and Pan American Copyright Conventions. No part of this book may be reproduced or transmitted in any form or by any means electronic or mechanical including photocopying and recording, or by any information storage and retrieval system, without permission in writing from the publisher.

www.AmiesPetCuisine.com

Printed in the United States. First revision 2008
Library of Congress Cataloging data.
Cousino, DVM, Amy.
Amies Pet Cuisine/Amy Cousino, DVM
Includes index. ISBN: 978-1-59872-943-6
1. Cooking. 2. Pet Food. I. How to Cook for Your Pet.

Printed in the United States of America

Contents

Introduction

I have been a veterinarian for nearly thirty years, and I cook professionally. I have advised thousands of people about their pets' diets. At first I recommended the standard commercial pet foods such as dry kibble, but I soon found that many ingredients used in those foods were unhealthy for my patients.

I started advising that they feed their pets' real foods in small quantities to improve the health of their pets. Soon I abandoned all commercial pet foods, stopped recommending them, and started my own pet food company, Amies Pet Cuisine.

By cooking for your pet, YOU control the quality of the food and, therefore, the safety of the food being fed. We must stop feeding by-products, additives, preservatives, artificial colorings, indigestible foods, and contaminated pet foods.

Homemade cooked pet meals are highly digestible and safe, which means they promote pet health. To make homemade organic pet food, simply use organic ingredients from your grocery store.

We must cook safe, wholesome, healthy homemade food for our pets because we want our pets to live long and feel well. They are a part of our families, and we love them.

How to Feed Your Pets

FEEDING ADULT DOGS

Adult dogs over one year old need at least two meals daily.

Give one serving every twelve hours, such as at 8:00 a.m. and 8:00 p.m. Then your dog will expect a meal at those times, making it efficient to take him/her outside to eliminate. Smaller dogs are more comfortable and less hungry with three or four small meals daily: split two servings into three to four portions.

If your dog gets hungry between meals, you may give him/her fruit or cooked vegetables. Leave the food down for no longer than fifteen minutes. Cover and refrigerate for later if not eaten within fifteen minutes.

The recipes in this cookbook should be made with fresh foods and stored in air-tight plastic containers. Use the food within three days if refrigerated and within three months if frozen.

FEEDING ADULT CATS

Like adult dogs, adult cats should also have scheduled meal-times. Feed two meals daily, giving one serving every twelve hours. Put your cat's food plate on top of a similar sized ice-filled bowl to keep the food cool. Discard any food not eaten within two hours.

Read above about food storage and preservation in the adult dog section above.

FEEDING PUPPIES AND KITTENS

Puppies and kittens need frequent meals four-to-six times daily. Schedule mealtimes and stick to them. Use the feeding guide included with these recipes for amounts. If your pup or kitten seems hungry between meals, feed him/her larger meals. Make sure to get your young pet to the veterinarian every two to three weeks for checkups, vaccinations, worming, and training instructions. A large, round, bloated belly, is often abnormal. Be sure to supervise kids who handle pups and kittens. Only adults should be responsible for feeding pets.

Cooking for Adult Dogs over Six Months Old

Cooking for dogs over one year old is easy. Before cooking, check the "No-No List" on page 54 in this book so that you do not include foods that are toxic, are indigestible, or that provoke illnesses. Del next phrase or will upset your dog's stomach.

Dogs have a shorter digestive tract than people, so they are much more sensitive to intense ingredients such as spices, and rich ingredients such as fats. Do not be creative. Follow these recipes exactly as written as you begin to cook for your dog. You will produce good, wholesome meals.

All recipes are intended for normal healthy dogs.

You should feed your dog two or three times daily and keep all food refrigerated in an airtight container for up to three days. You can also use vacuum-sealed bags to store meals in the freezer for up to three months. Frozen meals also travel well with lots of ice in a cooler or in a freezer on an RV or boat.

RECIPES FOR DOGS

Scrambled Eggs

2 eggs, slightly beaten
2 T. water
Pinch of Morton Lite salt
1/2 t. olive oil

Place a 7-inch sauté pan on low heat. Coat pan bottom with oil. In a small bowl, use a fork to whip eggs, water, and salt. Add eggs to pan. Stir with a wooden spoon until the eggs are cooked (curdled). Allow the eggs to cool before serving.

Feeding Guide for Dogs over Six Months Old

Breed Size	Servings
Toy or Small	2
Medium or Large	1
Giant	1/2

Feeding Guide for Cats Over Six Months Old

Breed Size	Servings
Adult Cats	2 to 3

Beef Pilaf for Dogs

1 lb. ground beef
1 T. olive oil
1/2 t. Morton Lite salt
1/8 t. oregano, dried
1 c. long-grain rice
Amie's Beef Broth, enough to moisten

Sauté beef in oil until brown and fully cooked. Cook rice (p. 13) separately.

In a large bowl, combine beef, rice, and oregano. While mixing, add broth as needed to moisten. Offer your dog cooked vegetables with this meal (see the "Yes-Yes List").

Slow cooker instructions: place all ingredients into a slow-cooker. Add 2 cups Amie's Beef Broth. Cover and cook on low 2 to 3 hours or until rice is tender and beef is fully cooked.

Feeding Guide for Dogs over Six Months Old

Breed Size	Servings
Toy	10 to 12
Small	8 to 10
Medium	6 to 8
Large	4 to 6
Giant	2 to 4

*Feed one full serving of this recipe twice daily.

Chicken Pilaf for Dogs

1 whole chicken breast, roasted

1 1/3 c. long-grain rice

Amie's Chicken Broth, enough to moisten

1/2 c. carrots, peeled, washed, diced and cooked

1 T. olive oil

Prepare the chicken (p. 14). Cook the rice (p. 13). Individual recipes will reference the page(s) for the basic component ingredients. Put the cooked chicken into a food processor and process into fine pieces. In a large bowl, fold together chicken and the rest of the ingredients.

While mixing, add broth as needed to moisten.

Feeding Guide for Dogs over Six Months Old

Breed Size	Servings
Toy	10 to 12
Small	8 to 10
Medium	6 to 8
Large	4 to 6
Giant	2 to 4

Tip: You may use the drippings from the roast chicken to improve the flavor.

Amie's Chicken Broth

1/2 whole chicken, cut into pieces
1/2 carrot, sliced
1/4 stalk celery, sliced
1/2 c. clam juice (opt.)
Water

Place all ingredients into a stockpot. Add water to just cover the chicken. Bring to a boil, then reduce heat; simmer uncovered for 20 to 30 minutes, until the chicken is fully cooked (no pink areas). Strain out all solid ingredients, reserving the broth. Use broth immediately or freeze it in ice cube trays. When frozen, remove cubes and store them in a labeled freezer bag until needed.

Safety Note: Do not use commercially made chicken, beef, or vegetable broths. They contain onions and garlic, which are both foods on the No-No List!

Amie's Beef Broth

1 lb. ground beef
1/2 carrot, peeled, trimmed, washed, and sliced
1/4 stalk celery, washed, and sliced
1/2 c. clam juice (opt.)
Water

Place all ingredients into a 2-qt. pot. Add enough water to just cover the beef. Bring to a boil, then immediately reduce the heat to low. Simmer uncovered for 20 minutes. Strain out all solid ingredients and reserve the broth.

Use the broth immediately or freeze it in ice cube trays. When frozen, remove cubes and store them in a labeled freezer bag until needed.

Rice

1 1/3 c. long-grain rice
3 c. water

Using a fine strainer, rinse rice until water is no longer cloudy after it runs over the rice. Put rice and water into a 2-qt. sauce pan on medium heat.

Bring rice to a boil. Immediately turn heat down to low and simmer, covered, for 15 minutes or until rice grains are soft. Remove from heat, drain off any remaining water, and allow to cool uncovered. Yields approx. 4 c.

Tip: To make the rice more flavorful, use Amie's Beef or Chicken Broth (p. 11) instead of plain water to cook the rice.

Roasted Chicken for Dogs or Puppies

1/2 chicken breast, with skin and bone
1/4 c. water

Preheat oven to 350 degrees. Place chicken into small roaster. Add water to pan. Roast uncovered 40 minutes—until meat juice is clear. Cool. Remove skin and bones. Chop meat into small dice.

Cooking Tip: You can also purchase a pre-roasted chicken from the supermarket. Make sure to get a plain, unseasoned chicken or a lemon-pepper chicken. Most of the seasoning is on the skin, so remove the skin and then use only the chicken meat for your recipe.

When using pre-cooked ingredients, always heed the No-No List.

Tacos for Dogs

1 lb. ground beef

1/8 t. oregano, dried

1 T. olive oil

1/2 t. Morton Lite salt

1/4 c. fresh tomato, peeled, seeded, and finely diced

1/2 c. romaine lettuce, washed and finely diced

1/4 c. mild cheddar cheese, finely shredded

4 small flour tortillas[*]

Sauté beef in olive oil until brown. Add tomatoes, oregano, and salt. Sauté until tomato is soft. To make tacos, place 1/4 of the meat onto a tortilla. Put 2 T. lettuce and 1 T. cheese on top of meat.

Fold taco in half. Slice taco into bite-sized pieces.

Feeding Guide for Dogs over Six Months Old

Breed Size	Number of Tacos Per Serving[a]
Toy	1
Small	2
Medium	3
Large	4 to 5
Giant	6 to 7

a. Feed one full serving twice daily.

---

[*] See the No-No List. Do not substitute corn taco shells or use spices.

Spaghetti and Meatballs for Dogs

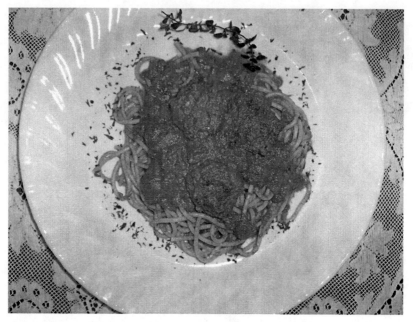

1 14-oz. can Hunt's diced tomatoes, unseasoned.

6 oz. ground beef

4 oz. Semolina spaghetti, broken into smaller pieces delete semolina altogether

1 T. olive oil

1/2 c. white, fresh bread crumbs

1/4 t. oregano, dried

2 Vigo brand sardines in tomato sauce, pureed

Combine beef, bread crumbs, and oregano. Form beef mixture into 6 meatballs. Sauté meatballs in olive oil until browned. Add tomatoes with their juice and sardines. Simmer sauce and meatballs, covered, 15 to 20 minutes.

Cook pasta in boiling water per label directions. Do not add salt. Drain pasta. Mix pasta and sauce together. Cool before serving. Yields 6 meatballs and about 8 oz. cooked pasta.

Feeding Guide for Dogs over Six Months Old

Breed Size	Serving Size
Toy	1 meatball, 1/4 c. sauce, 1 oz. spaghetti
Small	2 meatballs, 1/2 c. sauce, 2 oz. spaghetti
Medium	3 meatballs, 3/4 c. sauce, 4 oz. spaghetti
Large	4 meatballs, 1 c. sauce, 5 oz. spaghetti
Giant	Whole Recipe

Meatloaf and Mashed Potatoes for Dogs

Meatloaf:

1 lb. ground beef

1 egg, beaten

1/2 c. fresh white breadcrumbs

1 T. Amie's Beef Broth

1/2 t. Morton Lite salt

Preheat oven to 350 degrees. In a bowl, mix beef, egg, salt, broth, and crumbs. On a small baking sheet, mold mixture into a small loaf. Bake for 40 to 50 minutes or until meat juices from loaf are clear. Cool and cut into 4 slices.

Mashed Potatoes:

4 to 6 redskin potatoes

2 T. olive oil

1/4 t. salt, non-iodized

Water

Wash and trim potatoes. Slice them into 1/2-inch-thick rounds and put in sauce pan. Cover with water and bring to a boil over medium heat. Cook 10 minutes, covered, until tender. Drain potatoes, add salt and oil, and mash them.

Feeding Guide for Dogs over Six Months Old

Breed Size	Serving Size
Toy	1/4 to 1/2 slice meatloaf plus 1/8 to 1/4 c. mashed potatoes
Small	1/2 to 1 slice meatloaf plus 1/4 to 1/2 c. mashed potatoes
Medium	1 to 1-1/2 slice meatloaf plus 1/2 c. mashed potatoes
Large	2 slices meatloaf plus 1 c. mashed potatoes
Giant	2 to 4 slices meatloaf plus 1 to 2 c. mashed potatoes

Lamb Casserole for Dogs or Puppies

1 c. macaroni, cooked (use about 1/2 c. uncooked macaroni)
1 c. lamb, finely diced, browned in sauté pan
1/2 t. salt, non-iodized
1-1/2 c. milk
2 eggs, beaten

Butter a baking dish. Put macaroni in the dish. Mix lamb with salt and layer it over the macaroni. Mix the milk and eggs together and pour it over the meat. Bake at 350 degrees 25 to 35 minutes or until bubbly on the edges.

Feeding Guide for Dogs over Six Months Old

Breed Size	Serving Size
Toy	1/8 to 1/4 of this recipe
Small	1/4 recipe
Medium	1/2 recipe
Large	full recipe
Giant	double recipe

Beef Casserole for Dogs

Sauce:

2 T. olive oil

3 T. flour

1 1/2 c. Amie's Beef Broth

Heat the oil in a 1-qt. saucepan on medium heat. Add the flour and cook together for 1 minute; then add the broth and bring to a boil to thicken.

Filling:

2 c. macaroni, cooked (about 1 c. uncooked macaroni)

2 tomatoes, peeled, seeded, and diced

2 c. beef, ground, browned in sauté pan

Add macaroni, tomatoes, and beef to the casserole. Pour the sauce over and bake at 350 degrees for 25 to 35 minutes until edges are bubbly.

Feeding Guide for Dogs over Six Months Old

Breed Size	Serving Size
Toy	1/8 to 1/4 of this recipe
Small	1/4 recipe
Medium	1/2 recipe
Large	full recipe
Giant	double recipe

Southern Style Meatloaf for Dogs

2 c. ground beef, browned in sauté pan

3/4 c. long-grain rice

2 T. olive oil

2 T. flour

3/4 c. Amie's Beef Broth

In a large saucepan, mix the beef and the beef broth. Mix the oil and flour together, add to the pan and stir over medium heat until heated through and thickened.

Remove from heat. Cook the rice (p. 13). In a greased loaf pan, press half of the rice into a layer on the bottom. Add the beef mixture, and then top with a layer of rice.

Cover with foil and bake at 350 degrees for 35 minutes or until bubbly at the edges.

Feeding Guide for Dogs over Six Months Old

Breed Size	Serving Size
Toy	1/4 to 1/2 slice meatloaf
Small	1/2 to 1 slice meatloaf
Medium	1 to 1-1/2 slice meatloaf
Large	2 slices meatloaf
Giant	2 to 4 slices meatloaf

Beef Liver Pate for Dogs

1 c. bread crumbs

Milk or Amie's Beef Broth, enough to cover the crumbs

1 lb. beef liver

1 egg

1/2 t. salt, non-iodized

Put crumbs in a bowl and cover with milk or broth. Use a food processor to finely chop the liver. Drain the bread crumbs, saving the liquid. Add the crumbs and the egg to the liver, and process until combined. Move mixture to a bowl and slowly add reserved liquid, stirring until the liver mixture holds together.

Place in a greased pate pan and bake at 350 degrees for 1 hour. Cool and slice into 4 pieces.

Feeding Guide for Dogs over Six Months Old

Breed Size	Serving Size
Toy	1/2 slice
Small	1 slice
Medium	2 slices
Large	3 slices
Giant	Full recipe

Chicken Liver Pate for Dogs

1 c. bread crumbs

Milk or Amie's Chicken Broth, enough to cover the crumbs

1 lb. chicken livers

1 egg

1/2 t. salt, non-iodized

In a bowl, cover crumbs with milk or broth.

Use a food processor to finely chop the liver. Drain the bread-crumbs, saving the liquid. Combine the liver and bread crumbs. Move mixture to a bowl and slowly add reserved liquid until the liver mixture holds together. Place in a greased pate pan and bake at 350 degrees for 1 hour. Cool and slice into 4 slices.

Feeding Guide for Dogs over Six Months Old

Breed Size	Serving Size
Toy	1/2 slice
Small	1 slice
Medium	2 slices
Large	3 slices
Giant	Full recipe

Mashed Sweet Potatoes for Dogs or Puppies

2 sweet potatoes, peeled, trimmed, rinsed, and cut into 1/2-inch dice
Amie's Chicken or Beef Broth

Place the potatoes in a saucepan, covering with cold broth. Put a lid on the pan and bring to a boil over medium heat, cooking 15 to 20 minutes or until tender.

Drain potatoes, reserving the broth. Mash the potatoes, adding hot broth until potatoes are moist and hold together.

Feeding Guide for Dogs over Six Months Old
Feed as a side dish to meatloaf, cooked beef, or chicken.

How to Cook for Your Puppy

Your puppy needs good food for growth and good health. A homemade meal is far more digestible and wholesome than any kibble, pouch, or canned food you could buy.

Digestion is so important. Remember that pups are domesticated (not wild) and have been the companions of people for many thousands of years, so they are accustomed to eating our cooked foods. Raw meat, raw poultry, and raw fish are difficult to digest and can cause diarrhea, vomiting, malnutrition, or food poisoning.

Along with cooked foods, always give your pup a multi-vitamin-mineral tablet labeled "for puppies." Check the label against the No-No List, checking for ingredients not allowed.

Take your pup to your veterinarian every two to three weeks until he is four months old. After that, bring him to your veterinarian annually.

RECIPES FOR PUPPIES

Beef Pilaf for Puppies

1/2 c. long-grain rice
1 lb. ground beef
1 T. olive oil
1/2 c. carrots, peeled, washed, diced, and cooked
1/2 t. Morton Lite salt
Amie's Beef Broth, enough to moisten (p. 12)

Cook rice (p. 13). Sauté beef in olive oil until browned and fully cooked. Place beef in food processor with salt and process until finely minced. Add the rice and carrots to the processor. While the processor is running, gradually add broth until food is moistened and smooth.

Slow-cooker method:

Put all ingredients, including 1 c. of Amie's Beef Broth, into cooker. Cover and cook on low 2 to 3 hours or until rice is tender and beef is fully cooked. Add hot broth as needed during cooking to keep moist and stir occasionally to break up the meat.

Feeding Guide for Puppies up to Six Months Old

Breed Size	Serving Size*
Toy	1/4 c. to 1/2 c.
Small	1/3 c. to 2/3 c.
Medium	3/4 c. to 1 c.
Large	1-1/2 c. to 2 c.
Giant	1-3/4 c. to 2-1/2 c.

*Feed one serving 4 to 6 times daily, or every 4 to 6 hours.

Beefy Potatoes for Puppies

1 qt. redskin potatoes

2 T. olive oil

1/2 t. Morton Lite salt

1 lb. ground beef

1 T. olive oil

1 egg, hard-boiled

Amie's Beef Broth, enough to moisten

In a 2-qt. saucepan, cook the potatoes in water over medium heat until tender. Drain potatoes, mix in salt and oil, and mash them. Sauté the beef in 1 T. olive oil until browned and fully cooked. Place the beef, potatoes, and egg into a food processor and process into a smooth consistency, adding broth as needed to moisten.

Feeding Guide for Puppies up to Six Months Old

Breed Size	Serving Size*
Toy	1/4 to 1/2 c.
Small	1/3 to 2/3 c.
Medium	3/4 to 1 c.
Large	1-1/3 c.
Giant	1-1/2 c.

*Feed your puppy 4 to 6 servings per day or about 1 serving every 4 to 6 hours.

Chicken Pilaf for Puppies

2/3 c. long-grain rice
1/2 chicken breast, roasted
1 t. olive oil
Pinch of salt, non-iodized
Amie's Chicken Broth, enough to moisten (p. 11)

Prepare chicken (p. 14). Cook rice (p. 13). Place chicken, salt, and oil into food processor and process until finely minced. Add cooked rice. While processor is on, add broth slowly until food is smooth and moist.

Feeding Guide for Puppies up to Six Months Old

Breed Size	Serving Size[a]
Toy	1/4 to 1/2 c.
Small	1/3 to 2/3 c.
Medium	3/4 to 1 c.
Large	1–1/2 to 2 c.
Giant	1–3/4 to 2–1/2 c.

a. Feed one serving 4 to 6 times daily or every 4 to 6 hours.

Lamb Pilaf for Puppies

1/2 c. long-grained rice
1 lb. lamb, ground
1 T. olive oil
1/2 c. carrots, peeled, washed diced and cooked
1/2 t. Morton Lite salt
Amie's Beef Broth, enough to moisten

Cook rice (p. 13). Sauté lamb in olive oil until browned and fully cooked. Place lamb in food processor with salt and process until finely minced. Add the rice and carrots to the processor. Running the processor, gradually add broth until food is moistened and smooth.

Feeding Guide for Puppies up to Six Months Old

Breed Size	Serving Size
Toy	1/4 c. to 1/2 c.
Small	1/3 c. to 2/3 c.
Medium	3/4 c. to 1 c.
Large	1–1/2 c. to 2 c.
Giant	1–3/4 c. to 2–1/2 c.

Chicken Casserole for Dogs or Puppies

2 boneless, skinless chicken breasts, about 1 lb., cut into 1/2-inch cubes

Amie's Chicken Broth, enough to moisten

1 c. green beans, sliced small, cooked, or 1 c. carrots, diced fine, cooked

Hot chicken broth

Put chicken into a 1-qt. casserole, then add broth until chicken is just covered. Cover and bake at 350 degrees for 1/2 hour.

Remove from oven and add vegetables, mix together.

Feeding Guide for Puppies and Dogs

Breed Size	Serving Size for Puppies	Serving Size for Dogs
Toy or small	1/8 recipe	1/4 recipe
Medium	1/4 recipe	1/2 recipe
Large	1/2 recipe	whole recipe
Giant	whole recipe	double recipe

Boiled Chicken for Dogs or Puppies

1 chicken
Water
1/2 stalk celery, cut into 1-inch pieces
1/2 carrot, cut into 1-inch pieces
1 t. oregano, dried (optional)
1 t. rosemary, dried (optional)

Combine the chicken, vegetables, and optional seasonings in a 1-gallon pot. Add water to cover the chicken. Cover pot and bring to a boil. Immediately turn down the heat and simmer the chicken 45 minutes to 1 hour until tender. Skim foamy bits from the top of the water during cooking.

Remove chicken from pot and cool, then skin, bone, and cut meat into pieces. Store meat in an airtight container in the refrigerator up to 3 days. Use the chicken in recipes found in this cookbook. Use the broth in recipes now or preserve it by freezing it in ice cube trays. When frozen, put cubes into a clear freezer bag. Use the cubes in recipes calling for Amie's Chicken Broth. One cube = 1/4 c.

Easy Lamb Stew for Dogs or Puppies

2/3 c. long-grain rice

1 lb. ground lamb

1/2 c. carrots, diced and cooked

1/2 c. green beans, diced and cooked

Cooked peas, 1/2 c. (opt.)

1 c. Amie's Beef Broth (p. 12)

2 T. flour

Cook the rice (p. 13). Sauté the lamb until brown. Mix the flour into the lamb and cook 1 minute. Add the carrots, beans, and broth and stir to bring to a simmer. Simmer for 5 to 10 minutes. Stir rice into the meat and vegetables. If needed, add hot broth to moisten.

Feeding Guide for Puppies and Dogs over Six Months

Breed Size	Serving Size for Puppies	Serving Size for Dogs over Six Months
Toy	1/4 recipe	1/2 recipe
Small	1/4 recipe	1/2 recipe
Medium	1/2 recipe	1/2 recipe
Large	full recipe	double recipe
Giant	double recipe	quadruple recipe

Veal Patties for Dogs or Puppies

1 lb. ground veal
3 slices white bread
1 egg, beaten
Olive oil

Soak the bread in water. Squeeze the bread to remove the liquid and add to the veal and egg, mixing well.

Form into 4 patties. Heat the oil, then place patties in the pan.

Allow the first side to brown. Flip over and brown the other side. Cook until the juices coming from the meat are clear.

Feeding Guide for Puppies and for Dogs over Six Months

Breed Size	Serving Size for Puppies	Serving Size for Dogs over Six Months
Toy	1/4 patty	1/2 patty
Small	1/2 patty	1 patty
Medium	1 patty	2 patties
Large	2 patties	whole recipe
Giant	whole recipe	double recipe

Shepherd's Pie for Dogs or Puppies

1 lb. ground beef

1 qt. potatoes, peeled, trimmed, and quartered

1 T. olive oil

1/2 c. hot milk

1/2 c. carrots, diced, cooked

1/2 t. salt

2 c. Amie's Beef Gravy (p. 37)

Boil the potatoes until tender. Drain and put into a mixing bowl with the olive oil, milk, and salt.

Mash the potatoes. Cover and set aside. Sauté the beef until browned, then add gravy and carrots. Stir. Remove from heat. Preheat oven to 425 degrees. Place the beef mixture in an 8-inch-by-8-inch baking pan or casserole.

Spread mashed potatoes over the top evenly. Bake for 25 to 35 minutes until bubbly at the edges.

Feeding Guide for Puppies and for Adult Dogs

Breed Size	Serving Size for Puppies	Serving Size for Adult Dogs
Toy	1/4 c.	1/2 c.
Small	1/2 c.	2/3 c.
Medium	3/4 c.	1–1/2 c.
Large	1 c.	1–2/3 c.
Giant	1–1/2 c.	2 c.

Beef Gravy for Dogs or Puppies

2 T. olive oil
2 T. flour
1 c. Amie's Beef Broth

In a 1-qt. sauce pan, stir together the oil and flour over medium heat. Using a whisk to mix, slowly add the broth. Bring to a boil until thickened. Add more broth if needed to make a smooth, thick gravy. Simmer for 1 minute.

Feeding Guide for Dogs and Puppies
Use gravy in recipes and for topping meats or vegetables.

Chicken Gravy for Dogs or Puppies

2 T. olive oil
2 T. flour
1 c. Amie's Chicken Broth

In a 1-quart saucepan, mix the oil and flour over medium heat for 2 minutes. Stirring with a whisk, slowly add the broth. Bring to a boil, then turn down the heat to simmer. Add more broth if needed to make a smooth, thick gravy.

Feeding Guide for Dogs and Puppies
Use gravy in recipes and for topping meats or vegetables.

Cooking for Cats and Kittens

Cooking for cats and kittens is easy and fun. Cats prefer moist and finely textured meals. You'll need a food processor to cook their favorites. Since cats are domesticated animals, not wild, they digest cooked foods very well. Cats have problems digesting raw meat, fish, or poultry. Raw meat, fish, and poultry often cause indigestion and diarrhea, vomiting, or food poisoning.

Our domesticated pet cats are classified as obligate carnivores. This means they require only meat, fish, or poultry and fresh water to drink to meet their nutritional needs. Cats and kittens who do not eat these animal proteins become blind because of taurine deficiency before dying of malnutrition.

Cats make their own Vitamin C (so they are natural sailors, too, no scurvy!). Amie's recipes make very digestible meals, and this means a healthier cat or kitten. Read the No-No List on pages 54 to 57 before cooking.

A Special Note on Kittens

Take your kitten to your veterinarian every two to three weeks until he/she is three months old. Necessary examinations, vaccinations, and medications will be administered to your kitten so your kitten has a healthy start in life. Once your kitten is one year old, return to your veterinarian annually.

RECIPES FOR CATS AND KITTENS

Chicken or Turkey Giblets for Cats and Kittens

1/2 lb. fresh chicken or turkey giblets (excluding neck), rinsed and finely chopped

Amie's Chicken Broth (p. 11), enough to moisten.

Put the fresh giblets into a small saucepan. Add broth to just cover. Bring to a boil on medium heat. Turn the heat down and simmer, covered, about 30 minutes or until tender. Add hot broth as needed during cooking to keep giblets covered with liquid. Cool before serving.

Feeding Guide

Yields 3 servings for an adult cat, or 4 to 8 servings for kittens.

GRANDMA HAZEL'S STORY

Like many people in the early 1900s, my Grandma Hazel kept pet cats on her farm in Michigan. They were excellent mousers and beloved pets. Grandma cooked giblets for her cats to supplement their rodent diet.

Farm cats were essential to keeping the number of rodents down. Lucky kitties were they all. Now you can prepare this favorite for your own cats.

Salmon Pate for Cats and Kittens

4 oz. fresh salmon, poached (p. 47)

1/2 T. olive oil

1 egg, hard-boiled

Place all ingredients into a food processor. Process until smooth. Use some of the poaching liquid to moisten the food if needed.

Feeding Guide

Yields 3 servings for an adult cat, and 6 servings for kittens up to four months.

Safety Tip: Do not substitute smoked salmon: it contains preservatives that are harmful to your pet. Cats are very sensitive to chemicals. See the No-No List.

Tuna Pate for Cats and Kittens

1 6.5-oz. can tuna in water, drained.

1 T. olive oil

1 egg, hard-boiled

Place all ingredients in a food processor and process until smooth.

Feeding Guide

Yields 3 servings for an adult cat and 6 servings for kittens.

ANGEL'S STORY

Angel is my thirteen-year-old Manx cat. She is white with blue eyes. At the shelter where I met her, she had a large sign on her cage that stated "THIS CAT IS DEAF." No one wanted to adopt her, and she was due to be put to sleep in seven days. When I visited her, I talked to her and noted that, even though she sat facing the back of the cage, her ears moved when I spoke. I decided that she was not deaf, but that she was angry about being in the cage and ignoring all visitors. I adopted her, and over the next several years, Angel and I sailed together over 6,000 in all kinds of weather. She is a very good sailor, calm and rarely seasick. Each evening she would join me in the cockpit to sightsee. She even had the sense to have never jumped or fallen in the water. Tuna Pate is Angel's favorite meal, and I have been cooking it for her for years. She watches me cook and still listens to hear the spoon tapping the tuna onto her plate.

Beef Pate for Cats and Kittens

1 egg, hard-boiled
1 lb. ground beef (or ground lamb)
1/2 T. olive oil
Amie's Beef Broth (p. 12), enough to moisten

Sauté beef until brown and fully cooked.

Put beef, egg, and oil into food processor and blend until finely minced. While processor is running, add broth until pate is moist and smooth.

Feeding Guide

Kittens up to six months old—18 servings (serving size: 1/2 to 1 oz.)

Cats— 9 servings (serving size 2 oz.)

KITTY'S STORY

Kitty was the first cat I met when I moved into my home in Charleston, South Carolina. She was a black female with green eyes and a scraggly, flea-bitten fur coat. Each time I left or returned home, Kitty would come running, and I would pet her and pick her up.

She was so docile and friendly that the neighbors all knew and loved her, too. Some of us fed her, since her owner was ill and rarely let Kitty indoors. Kitty loved beef pate, which I fed her often. I treated her flea problem, too, so after a few weeks, her fur was shiny and beautiful, and she was healthy again.

Poached Salmon for Cats and Kittens

4 oz. fresh salmon

Clam juice, 8 oz., or Amie's Chicken Broth (p. 11), 8 oz.

Put clam juice (or broth) into a small saucepan. Bring to a boil on medium heat, covered. Add salmon and immediately reduce heat. Cover and poach for 10 to 15 minutes or until salmon flakes easily.

Remove salmon to a clean plate. Flake the salmon apart with a fork, removing bones.

Feeding Guide

Yields 2 servings for an adult cat or 4 to 8 servings for kittens.

Tip: You can cook fresh tuna in the same manner. Do not add salt to the poaching liquid.

Chicken Pilaf for Cats and Kittens

1 whole chicken breast, roasted
2/3 c. long-grain rice
2 eggs, hard-boiled
Amie's Chicken Broth (p. 11), enough to moisten

Prepare the chicken (p. 14). Cook rice (p. 13). Put cooked chicken, rice, and eggs into a food processor and process into fine pieces. Add broth as needed to moisten into a smooth mixture.

Feeding Guide
Yields 6 2-oz. servings for an adult cat or 12 1-oz. servings for kittens.

Tip: Use the drippings from roasting the chicken to intensify the chicken flavor.

Tuna Soufflé for Cats and Kittens

2 c. tuna, poached, flaked, and deboned
1/2 c. white, unseasoned bread crumbs
1/2 c. milk
3 egg yolks, beaten until thickened
3 egg whites, beaten to hard peaks
Water

Put the milk and bread crumbs into a 1-qt. saucepan.

Cook on medium heat until heated through. Off the heat, gradually stir in the egg yolks and tuna. Fold in the egg whites. Grease an 8-inch-×-8-inch casserole and pour tuna mixture into it. Set it into a larger baking pan.

Pour boiling water into the larger pan up to half the depth of the soufflé mixture. Put into the oven and bake at 350 degrees for 25 to 30 minutes or until firm.

Feeding Guide
Yields 8 servings for cats, 16 servings for kittens.

Salmon Soufflé for Cats and Kittens

2 c. salmon, poached, flaked, and deboned
1/2 c. bread crumbs
1/2 c. milk
3 egg yolks, beaten until thickened
3 egg whites, beaten to hard peaks

Put the milk and crumbs into a 1-qt. saucepan. Cook on medium heat until heated through. Turn off the heat gradually stir in the egg yolks and salmon. Fold in the egg whites. Grease an 8-inch-×-8-inch casserole. Pour the salmon mixture into it. Set it into a larger baking dish. Pour boiling water into the larger pan—not into the salmon casserole—up to half the depth of the salmon mixture.

Bake at 350 degrees for 25 to 30 minutes or until firm.

Feeding Guide
Yields 8 servings for cats and 16 servings for kittens.

Salmon Loaf for Cats and Kittens

1 c. salmon, poached (p. 47), flaked, and deboned
1/2 c. bread crumbs
1 egg
1 T. olive oil

Put all ingredients into a food processor. Process until creamy and smooth. Grease a mini loaf pan or small ovenproof bowl with olive oil. Pour in the salmon mixture.

Place the loaf pan into a larger casserole. Pour boiling water into the larger casserole, up to half the depth of the salmon mixture. Bake at 350 degrees for 20 to 25 minutes or until firm.

Feeding Guide
Yields 8 servings for cats and 16 servings for kittens.

Tuna Balls for Cats and Kittens

4 oz. tuna, poached, flaked and deboned, reserving poaching liquid, (p. 47)

1 egg, beaten

1/4 c. long-grain or sushi rice

Cook the rice (p. 13), then cool to room temperature. Combine the rice, tuna, and egg. Make into 6 balls. Bring the reserved poaching liquid to a boil. Drop in the balls.

Cover, reduce heat to low, and simmer for 10 minutes. Remove from heat, leave covered, and steep 15 more minutes.

Feeding Guide
Yields 2 servings for cats and 4 servings for kittens.

Salmon Balls for Cats and Kittens

4 oz. salmon, poached, flaked, and deboned, reserving poaching liquid (p. 47)

1 egg, beaten

1/2 T. olive oil

1/4 c. long-grain or sushi rice

Cook the rice (p. 13) and cool to room temperature. Mix the rice, salmon, egg, and oil and form 6 balls. Bring the reserved poaching liquid to a boil. Add the balls, cover, and reduce heat to low. Simmer for 10 minutes.

Remove from heat, leave covered, and steep for 15 minutes.

Feeding Guide
Yields 2 servings for cats, 4 servings for kittens.

No-No List

Clockwise from left: spices, soup, sausage, coffee, onion, garlic, hot sauce, chocolate, condiments.

Never feed any food or ingredient listed here to your dog, puppy, cat, or kitten. See the key at the bottom of this table for the meaning of the numbers.

Meats	
Pork, ham, prosciutto, hot dogs	1, 2, 3
Sausage, kielbasa, brats, etc.	2, 3
Chicken, beef, or vegetable broth or stock	1, 2, 3
Bouillon cubes or granules	1, 2, 3
Ribs	1, 2, 3

Jerky strips	1, 2, 3
Pizza	1, 2, 3
Bacon, Canadian bacon	1, 2, 3
Beef by-products	1, 2, 3
Chicken by-products	1, 2, 3
Other by-products	1, 2, 3
Vegetables and Fruits	
Broccoli	1
Rhubarb	2
Collards	1, 2
Peppers: green, banana, jalapeno, habañero, red bell, etc.	1, 2
Garlic	1*
Garlic oil	1*
Raisins and grapes	1
Mushrooms	1
Onions, chives, shallots, or any foods containing these	1, 2*
Corn: on the cob, kernels, taco shells and chips, corn-meal, Cheetos, polenta, grits, or any foods containing corn	2*
Potato chips	2, 3
Popcorn	2, 3
Seasonings	
Black pepper	2
Salt, iodized	1, 3
Cayenne, paprika, cinnamon, allspice, five-spice powder, etc.	2

Ketchup, catsup, tomato sauce (those containing seasonings)	1, 2
Mustards: hot Chinese, yellow, dry	2
Fermented sauces (soy sauce, fish sauce)	1
Salad dressings, pickles	1, 2, 3
Barbecue sauce, hot sauce	1, 2, 3
Chemicals	
Preservatives: BHT, EDTA, Ethoxyquin, etc.	1, 3
Miscellaneous	
Peanut Butter	***
Beer	1, 2
Wine	1, 2, 3
Alcoholic beverages	1, 2, 3
Marijuana	1, 3
Drugs *not prescribed* by a licensed veterinarian	1
Vitamins labeled for humans with more than 200 percent of ADR	1, 2, 3
Chocolate: all kinds, foods containing chocolate or cocoa	1
Canned soups	1
Bones: all kinds, no exceptions	2
Greenies	2
Dog/cat treats	1, 2, 3
Pickles	1, 2
Fried food	2
Bacon fat: raw, cooked, or rendered	1, 2, 3
Pig ears, hooves	1, 2, 3***

Lard	2
Candy	2, 3
Cheese with veins: blue, Roquefort, etc.	1, 2
Brie rind	1
Almonds	1
Xylitol containing chewing gum	1
Prepared or processed foods containing anything on this list. This includes dry pet food kibble and canned or pouch pet foods.	1, 2, 3, ***, *

Key

1=Toxic
2=Indigestible or stomach/bowel irritant, provokes illness
3=Chemical additives
*Check your "Gourmet" dog biscuits—MOST have garlic or garlic oil in them. All forms of garlic are toxic to pets.
**In addition, do not feed your pet from plastic food or water dishes, they are toxic to pets. This is especially important for cats and kittens. Use stainless steel, china, or stoneware dishes instead. Use clean dishes daily: use the dishwasher or hand wash with Dawn detergent, then scald with boiling water. Dry with clean dishcloth.
***May contain bacteria responsible for food poisoning such as *Salmonella, E. Coli,* and *Campylobacter.* Foods and non-food items poisonous to humans are poisonous to pets also.

Yes-Yes List

Clockwise from left: beans, peas, carrot, tomato, orange, basil, half and half, banana, rice, rosemary, olive oil, Swiss cheese, cheddar cheese, parsley, lima beans.

This is a list of foods you may feed your dog, puppy, cat, or kitten safely:

Vegetables, cooked, preferably salt free

Vegetables, fresh, cut up into dice or shredded. Wash and trim first.

Fruits, fresh or cooked. Remove seeds, pits, spoiled parts, stems, and leaves.

Beef, meat only, cooked only

Veal, meat only, cooked only

Chicken, meat or giblets, no necks, cooked

Chicken fat, small amounts, rendered from cooking*

Turkey, meat or giblets, no necks, cooked

Tuna, fresh or canned, cooked

Salmon, fresh, cooked

Cornish hen, meat only, cooked

Duck, meat only

Rice, long-grain, short-grain

Pasta, made with semolina flour only

Potatoes, cleaned, trimmed of eyes, green areas, rotten areas

Sweet potatoes, cleaned and trimmed, as potatoes above

Cheese, cheddar, mozzarella

Cream, half and half, small amounts

Note: Do not give your pet any of these foods if they have been fried or seasoned with spices, pepper, or iodized salt, or if they also contain foods from the No-No List (p. 54).

*Meats, fish, and poultry must be fully cooked. Always use unspoiled foods—if it smells bad, pitch it.

How to Season Your Pet's Food

Dogs and cats have a more sensitive sense of smell than people, so you should use much smaller amounts of seasoning than when you're cooking for people.

It is likely your pet will not even notice that you didn't add additional seasoning. He will just be delighted to eat your homemade diet. But creative cooks can safely use these flavor enhancers:

Amie's Beef or Chicken Gravy
Oregano,
Rosemary (minced),
Parsley
Dill,
Basil
Salt, non-iodized
Morton Lite salt
Sardines, Vigo, pureed, canned, in tomato sauce
Clam juice
Amie's Chicken Broth or Beef Broth

Clams, canned, pureed

Tomato sauce: Check label carefully. *Must not contain onion, garlic, or spices. See No-No List. Consider making your own sauce.*

Olive oil

Fresh lemon, lime, or orange juice

Butter, real, and in small amounts only

Hunt's, canned, small diced tomatoes: *Run through processor, before using.*

Recommended Equipment and Food and Supplement Sources

EQUIPMENT

Small and large food processors

Seal-a-Meal® or FoodSaver® vacuum-packaging machine with
  bags

Stock pot

Sauce pans: 1 qt, and 2 qt.

Mixing bowl: 2 qt.

Knives: French and paring

Cutting board (wooden)

Colander or strainer

Air-tight plastic food containers

Cooking utensils, assorted spoons, whisks

Slow-cooker (optional)

Measuring cups

Scale

Measuring spoons

FOOD AND SUPPLEMENT SOURCES

All foods used in these recipes can be purchased at grocery stores. It is recommended that you also give your pet a multivitamin-mineral supplement that can be purchased from your veterinarian.[*]

INTERNET: WWW.AMIESPETCUISINE.COM

Multivitamins, supplements, cookbooks, flea prevention products*

---

[*] Always check the freshness date and the ingredients. (Make sure to not give any product with ingredients on the No-No List).

Favorite Foods
Questionnaire

Make a copy of this page for each of your pets before filling it out.

Fill out this form according to your observations of your pet. Don't leave anything off the list. After making the list, cross off any foods that are on the No-No List, and never feed them again.

Use this list to serve as a guide. For example, if your dog likes beef, cook the Beef Pilaf to start.

Foods that (pet's name) _____ likes to eat:

_____   _____

_____   _____

_____   _____

_____   _____

_____   _____

_____   _____

Now, list the recipes you have made for your pet, noting his/her favorites:

_____   _____

_____   _____

_____   _____

_____   _____

_____   _____

_____   _____

Index

CPSIA information can be obtained at www.ICGtesting.com
Printed in the USA
LVOW081142140312

273036LV00001B/262/P